HAVE A positive IMPACT...

...ON Yourself

by Hermione Redshaw

KidHaven PUBLISHING

Published in 2025 by
KidHaven Publishing, an Imprint of
Greenhaven Publishing, LLC
2544 Clinton St., Buffalo, NY 14224

Written by: Hermione Redshaw
Edited by: Robin Twiddy
Designed by: Amy Li

Cataloging-in-Publication Data

Names: Redshaw, Hermione, 1998-.
Title: On yourself / Hermione Redshaw.
Description: Buffalo, New York : KidHaven Publishing, 2025. | Series: Have a positive impact... | Includes glossary and index.
Identifiers: ISBN 9781534547551 (pbk.) | ISBN 9781534547568 (library bound) | ISBN 9781534547575 (ebook)
Subjects: LCSH: Self-acceptance--Juvenile literature. | Self-confidence--Juvenile literature. | Self-esteem--Juvenile literature.
Classification: LCC BF575.S37 R48 2025 | DDC 158.1--dc23

Manufactured in the United States of America

CPSIA compliance information: Batch #CSKH25
For further information contact Greenhaven Publishing LLC at 1-844-317-7404.

Please visit our website, www.greenhavenpublishing.com.
For a free color catalog of all our high-quality books, call toll free 1-844-317-7404 or fax 1-844-317-7405.

Find us on

Contents

Words that look like this are explained in the glossary on page 31.

Who ARE You?

You are yourself. You are unique, meaning there is no one else in the whole world like you. You have a unique personality, thoughts, and experiences. These are a large part of what makes you who you are.

Everyone has their own unique self. Your friends and family all have their own thoughts and experiences. Some might be similar to yours. Others might be completely different.

HAVE YOU EVER THOUGHT ABOUT THE THINGS THAT MAKE YOU DIFFERENT FROM THE PEOPLE YOU KNOW?

It is important to take care of yourself. When things start to get out of control and you feel stressed, it can start to impact you in a negative way.

Make time for you. Learn how to take care of yourself the way you would take care of others. This will help you to have a positive impact on yourself.

Being the Best You

What sort of person do you want to be when you grow up? Do you want to be kind? Clever? The sort of person who gets things done?

The things that we do now will shape the person we will become later in life. The lessons we learn while we are young will stay with us. So, the person you want to be tomorrow starts with who you are today!

How can reading a book help you to be the best you? This book is a starting point. It will offer you some direction and tips. It will also teach you some skills that will help you start your lifelong journey of positivity.

Understanding who we are and what we do is an important step. Learning helps us grow as people. What you learn about here will become tools that you can draw upon to help you for the rest of your life.

Mindfulness

Mindfulness means paying full attention to something, or slowing down to really notice what you are doing. When you are mindful, you are focusing in a relaxed way. You are not trying to rush or focus on lots of things at once.

Sometimes, mindfulness happens naturally. When you are doing something that you are good at and enjoy, you might find that your mind is focused completely on the task and nothing else. This might happen when you are playing an instrument or making art..

Being mindful can help us to cope with stress and manage our emotions. It can also help us to build our confidence and relate to others in difficult moments.

THIS GIRL IS BEING MINDFUL TO HELP HER FRIEND.

How to Be Mindful

Mindfulness is all about focus. Try these techniques:

+ Focus on your breathing. Notice how your stomach moves with each breath. Count as you breathe in and breathe out.

+ Think about something you find difficult. How does it make you feel? What could you do to turn the negative bits into something positive?

Mental Hygiene

Much like we would take care of a car, our homes, or our bodies, we have to take care of our minds to keep them running. Regular checks can help a car run smoothly with fewer issues, and the same goes for your mind.

Mental hygiene is all about looking after our minds. What you put in is what you get out. Fill your mind with positive things that are good for you and you will feel positive in your day-to-day life.

These are just a few things that can help to keep our minds healthy:

+ Eating healthy food
+ Getting regular exercise
+ Having time and freedom to play
+ Resting and relaxing

Mental health is how well we feel in our minds. It can be common for lots of people to experience mental health issues. Talking with people you trust about how you are feeling can help.

Managing Emotions

Emotions, whether good or bad, can be overwhelming at times. Have you ever felt so sad that you couldn't stop crying, or angry enough to start screaming? Maybe you have laughed so hard that your stomach hurt, or smiled so much that your cheeks became sore.

"IF YOU DON'T MANAGE YOUR EMOTIONS, THEN YOUR EMOTIONS WILL MANAGE YOU."

Learning to recognize your emotions and understanding why you are feeling them can help you manage them. It is important to feel emotions, but managing emotions can help stop them getting in your way.

Think about the last time you felt a strong emotion. What caused you to feel it? We can't always remove the cause, but we can control how we respond to it.

Everyone feels emotions slightly differently. Try talking to others about what makes them feel more angry, sad, or happy than normal. Talking about your emotions with someone else can often help to calm your mind.

SOMETIMES, DISTRACTING YOURSELF WITH A POSITIVE EMOTION CAN HELP TO MANAGE THE NEGATIVE ONES.

Learning FROM Mistakes

Everybody makes mistakes. Sometimes it can feel like we make lots of mistakes. However, mistakes are how we learn. The most successful people learn from mistakes to become the best at what they do.

Do not be ashamed of making a mistake. Knowing you did something wrong is the key to doing it right the next time. Making a mistake is not failing if you learn from your experience.

Creative people can have failures. Famous <u>authors</u>, actors, and musicians will be told their work is not good enough many times before they succeed. Sometimes, they make changes to make it better. However, someone else might like their work exactly as it is.

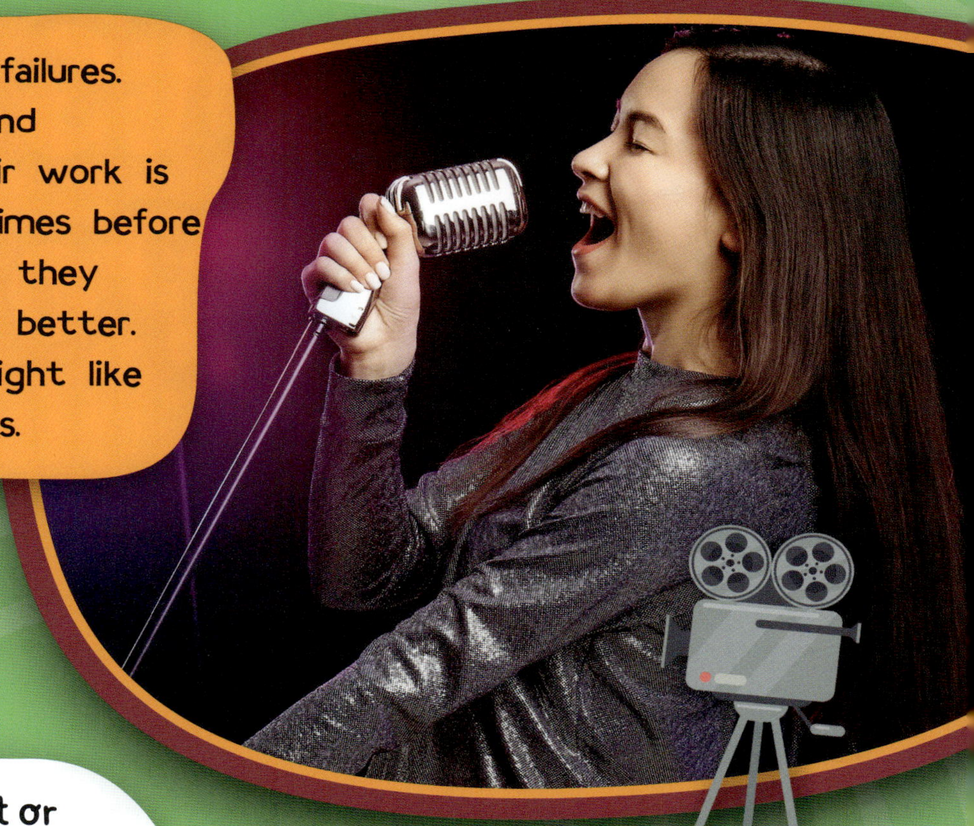

When there is no clear right or wrong, to say something is "good" or "bad" is just an opinion. Opinions vary from person to person, but the opinions of others can sometimes influence our own thoughts. Have faith in your abilities and learn what makes you proud of yourself.

GRANDMA DID NOT LIKE THE FILM, BUT THE KIDS LOVED IT! THEIR OPINIONS ARE DIFFERENT.

Benefits of Being Positive

Positivity is a mental attitude that means you are viewing things and situations in a good or constructive way. Positive thinking is a powerful tool to help you cope with and build resilience to difficult or stressful situations.

Being positive does not mean ignoring the negatives in life. It can be good to accept a negative situation or feeling. Then, try to see it in a way that is positive or useful.

WHAT CAN YOU LEARN FROM IT? FOCUS ON THE GOOD PARTS.

Have you ever lost at a game or competition? You can sometimes feel sad that you did not win, even if you came second. However, there are positives to be found. Try to focus on how much fun you had while playing and competing.

Professional athletes go through this all the time. Not everyone can win in a competition, yet many people can take part. Athletes often congratulate each other at the end of their competition, even if they did not win.

Role Models

We learn how to act by watching what others do. However, not everyone we meet acts in a way that we like. People we look up to are called role models, and it is important to find good role models in our lives.

Good role models will be people who have qualities you would like to see in yourself. Perhaps you want to be kind, polite, or a good speaker and know someone who you think is good at those things.

Think of someone who you might look up to. What is it about them that makes them worthy of being a role model? Look at how they tackle situations and think about how things in their life might have led them to be the person they are now.

Think about a negative situation you have been in. What would your role model have done?

Role models are not people we try to copy exactly. Instead, they help us to become better versions of ourselves. So, what qualities do you like about yourself? Does your role model have those qualities, too?

Self-Image

Just as it is good to think positively about negative situations, it is good to think positively about ourselves.

YOU CAN DO IT!

REMEMBER, THERE IS ONLY ONE YOU. THAT MAKES YOU PRETTY SPECIAL!

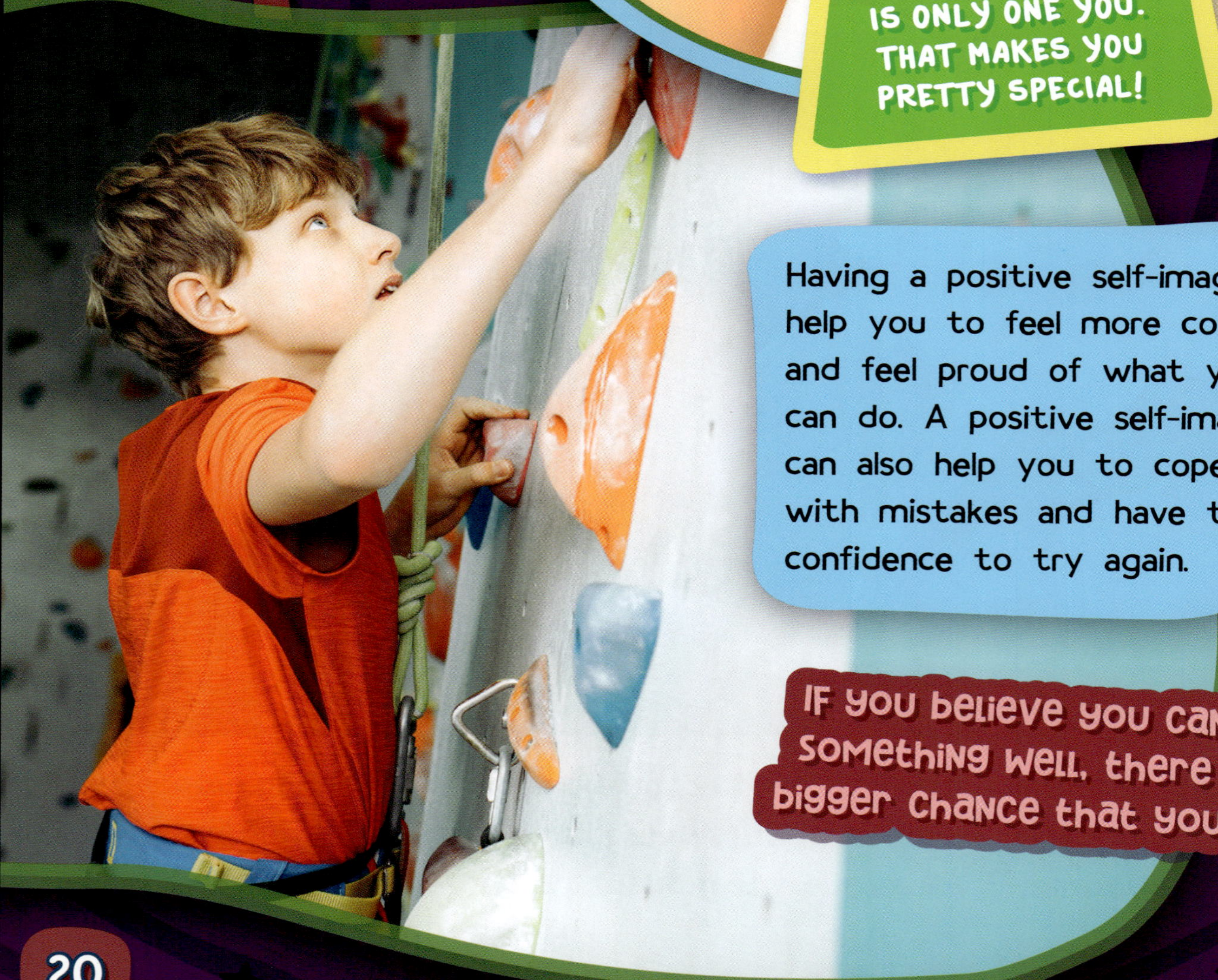

Having a positive self-image can help you to feel more confident and feel proud of what you can do. A positive self-image can also help you to cope with mistakes and have the confidence to try again.

IF YOU BELIEVE YOU CAN DO SOMETHING WELL, THERE IS A BIGGER CHANCE THAT YOU WILL!

Sometimes, we do not feel so good about ourselves. This can happen when we compare ourselves to others. It is important to remember that no two people are the same. You might not be as good as someone else at one thing, but you might be better at something else.

Sometimes, we can feel bad when we compare ourselves to who we want to be. It is okay to want to be better as a person. However, it is most important to be happy with who you are.

Try drawing yourself. Write around it the positive qualities you have.

If you do not think you have a positive self-image, it is important to develop one. Instead of focusing on what you think is wrong or bad about yourself, think about your positive points and things you have done right or well.

What do you do if you are struggling to think of positives? If you are stuck thinking about the negatives, try to think about how you can turn those negatives into positives.

One way to turn negatives into positives is to make changes. Perhaps you have said or done something that you wish you had not. Think about why you did what you did. We cannot change what happened, but we can learn how to do better next time.

IF WE UNDERSTAND WHY WE DO THINGS, WE CAN WORK ON CHANGING THEM.

Sometimes, what we think is a negative might actually be a positive. Some people might think being stubborn is a negative. However, stubborn people can also be determined, meaning they will not give up. This can be a good thing.

THE Power OF Good Habits

Habits are things that we do all the time without thinking about it. The habits we learn when we are young, whether good or bad, can stay with us throughout our lives. This is why it is important to learn good habits as soon as we can.

"WE ARE WHAT WE REPEATEDLY DO."

The Science Behind Habits

LEARNING GOOD HABITS IS JUST AS IMPORTANT AS NOT LEARNING BAD HABITS.

Trying to do new things is not always an easy task. That is because our brains have to send messages from one part of our brain to another. When we do the same thing often, our brains know what to do and find it easier to send these messages again.

Adding exercise to our routines can help to keep us healthy. It might be hard at first, but if you exercise at the same time every day, your mind and body will quickly get used to it. In fact, after you have been doing it for a while, your body and mind will expect it.

We can even train our brains to get in the mood for whatever positive habit we are forming. Try listening to the same piece of music every time you start your new activity. Soon, hearing that music will make you want to do the activity.

THE Power OF Language

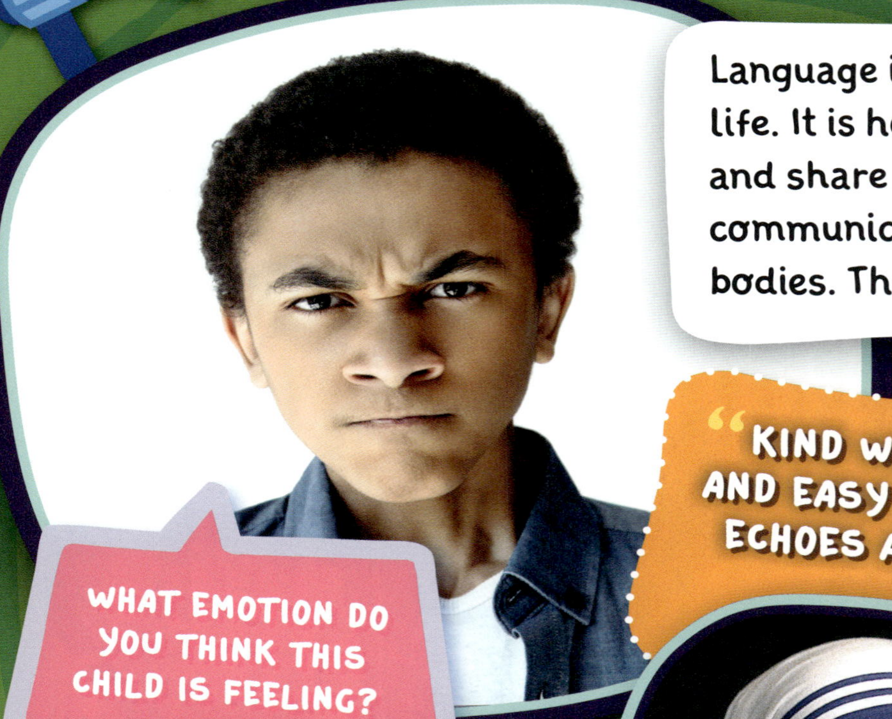

Language is a huge part of everyday life. It is how we talk to each other and share our thoughts. We can also communicate emotions using our bodies. This is called body language.

WHAT EMOTION DO YOU THINK THIS CHILD IS FEELING?

"KIND WORDS CAN BE SHORT AND EASY TO SPEAK, BUT THEIR ECHOES ARE TRULY ENDLESS."

– MOTHER TERESA

The types of language we use can have an impact on how we think, feel, and act. Even when words mean similar things, choosing one over another can change the meaning of what you say.

Positive language can go a long way. It is good to think about how you can use language to turn a negative into a positive. For example, instead of saying, "I failed," you could say, "I made some mistakes that I will try not to make again."

Individual words can have a big impact, too. Some words can have a negative and a positive meaning. If you are feeling tired, you are not being "lazy." If you can imagine something others find difficult to believe, you are not "crazy." Think about how you can use language positively to help yourself.

Mind AND Body

Our minds and our bodies are connected. What we do with our bodies can have an impact on how we feel. Both need to be looked after in order for us to be happy and healthy.

"THE MIND AND BODY ARE NOT SEPARATE. WHAT AFFECTS ONE AFFECTS THE OTHER."

HAS YOUR STOMACH EVER FELT WEIRD WHEN YOU STAND IN FRONT OF A BIG CROWD?

If we are sick, we can feel unhappy. If we are unhappy, we can also feel sick.

The mind and body connection works just the same with positivity. It is important to make healthy lifestyle choices to look after your mind and body. Exercising and eating well can improve your mood as well as make you stronger and healthier.

If you are happy, your body will feel happy, too. If your body is healthy, your mind will also be healthy.

Look after both your mind and your body and you will feel super!

Having a positive impact on yourself can help many things in your life. Just as your mind is connected to your body, your actions are connected to your important relationships.

Learning to manage your emotions can help you to stop negative thinking that can make you unwell. Having a positive self-image can make you feel more confident. That confidence will help you to be the best you possible!

Glossary

athletes	people who take part in sports
authors	people who write books
constructive	helpful to someone instead of upsetting and negative
lifestyle	a person's way of living
qualities	features that something or someone has
resilience	the ability to become strong or healthy after something bad happens
techniques	special ways of doing things

Index

Image Credits

All images are courtesy of Shutterstock.com, unless otherwise specified. With thanks to Getty Images, Thinkstock Photo and iStockphoto. Recurring images – imagewriter. Cover – ESB Professional, Evgeniya Sheydt, irin-k, Marek Mnich, monticello, pixfly. 2–3 – MonkeyBusinessImages. 4–5 – Mascha Tace, fizkes, Khosro, Bao zhonghui, monticello, irin-k. 6–7 – Modvector, Mascha Tace, GoodStudio, Brocreative, imtmphoto, Veronica Louro, wavebreakmedia. 8–9 – Pavel Savchuk, Boyko.Pictures, Littlekidmoment Raywoo, SeventyFour, Torychemistry. 10–11 – BearFotos, fizkes, FXQuadro, Jr images, kaisorn, Tartila. 12–13 – Indian concepts, Inside Creative House, Khosro, Maryna_Auramchuk, Yefym Turkin. 14–15 – Somchai Som, BRO.vector, Just dance, Monkey Business Images, N U S A R A, Pixel-Shot, Studio_G. 16–17 – Alexander_Safonov, azure1, CGN089, Focus_Vector, Pressmaster, True Touch Lifestyle, Vector Goddess. 18–19 – 1981 Rustic Studio kan, Alena Ozerova, antoniodiaz, GoodStudio, pixelheadphoto digitalskillet, SeventyFour. 20–21 – GoodStudio, Focus_Vector, George Rudy, Krakenimages.com, Larisa Tyushova, Soloviova Liudmyla, Vorobyeva woocat. 22–23 – 4zevar, eamesBot, Krakenimages.com, myboys.me, stockfour, YAKOBCHUK VIACHESLAV. 24–25 – Alena Ozerova, allensima, BorisShevchuk, DashaKos, Prostock-studio, Tartila, YanLev. 26–27 – CREATISTA, JIR Moronta, LightField Studios, mark reinstein], Rido, Guppic the duck, wavebreakmedia. 28–29 – allensima, BGStock72, Blueastro, Krakenimages.com, Maks Narodenko Oqvector, Prostock-studio, ShlyahovaYulia. 30 – Ground Picture, Max kegfire, Tartila.